SUN VALLEY SIGNATURES III

A PHOTOGRAPHIC PORTRAIT OF THE SUN VALLEY AREA

Photography by David R. Stoecklein

ISBN 0-922029-00-8

Publisher: David R. Stoecklein
Photographer: David R. Stoecklein
Designer/Typographer: Typographics, Ketchum, Id.
Color Separations/Printing: Sun Litho, Salt Lake City, UT

All photos in this book are available in original signed prints.
Please write or call:

David R. Stoecklein
P.O. Box 856
Ketchum, Idaho 83340
208-726-5191
800-727-5191

ACKNOWLEDGEMENTS

I could not do this book or any other photography project without the loving support of my beautiful wife, Mary, or my three naughty boys Drew, Taylor and Colby.

I would like to give special thanks to my team: Gretchen Palmer, Steve Mason, Kris Olenick and Wendy Carter who style models, organize the shoots, edit the film and organize the office. They keep me, and most of all, my clients happy. Thanks guys, I couldn't have done it without you.

F O R W A R D

Sun Valley casts a spell that inspires people to give up lucrative jobs in the city for a lifestyle weighted heavily toward recreation and the outdoors. It can also drive a first-time visitor straight to a real estate office in search of a cabin in the Sawtooths, a home in Ketchum, or a condominium in Sun Valley. This feeling overtook me in 1970 on my first visit to Sun Valley, but I didn't move here until 1979 when I decided that of all the ski resorts I had worked or lived in, Sun Valley was the best to raise a family.

To most of us who live or vacation here, Sun Valley is much more than a resort. It's a great environment with recreational opportunities—a playground, if you will—that is a driving force in our lives.

Within the confines of the Wood River Valley, you can wear yourself ragged with all the possibilities. In the winter you can Alpine ski on Baldy, cross-country ski at Galena, stay at a yurt in the Pioneers or snowmobile up Baker Creek. When the snows leave, there's tennis, swimming, golf, mountain biking, fishing, hunting, horseback riding and much much more.

Expand the playground to include everything accessible within a one hour drive in any direction and you have world-class hunting and fishing on the Snake, Little Wood and Big Lost rivers; hiking and camping in the Pioneer, Sawtooth, or White Cloud mountains; windsurfing and water-skiing at Magic Reservoir; or kayaking and rafting on the Snake, Salmon and Payette rivers.

If it's the recreation and natural beauty that puts us under that Sun Valley spell, it's the warm and friendly people that keep us enchanted. The grand mosaic of ranchers, stock brokers, carpenters, river guides, athletes, restaurant workers and artists all living together in pursuit of a healthy, outdoor lifestyle with room for individuality.

This book is for you, the people of the Wood River Valley. I hope it helps you recall the feeling that you first experienced here, and that it makes you want to get out and continue discovering the beauty of our valley.

David R. Stoecklein

DEDICATION

I would like to dedicate Sun Valley Signatures III to the memory of Lane Parrish.

Lane was always the first in the lift line on a powder morning and the last off the mountain. Most of all he was the first to help a friend in need. Lane never forgot his friends and we'll never forget him.

Thanks Lane, for all your help. We miss you.

LANE PARRISH, SKIING HIS FAVORITE SPOT,
THE BACKSIDE OF WARM SPRINGS
Plate 1

SUN VALLEY OPERA HOUSE
Plate 2

SUN VALLEY LAKE
Plate 3

BACKSIDE OF DOLLAR MOUNTAIN
Plate 5

BACKSIDE OF DOLLAR MOUNTAIN
Plate 6

SKIING RIDGE
Plate 7

SKIING THE BOWLS
Plate 4

SNOWCAT PREPARES THE CROSS COUNTRY
TRACKS ON THE SUN VALLEY GOLF COURSE
Plate 8

OLD MILK BARN ON SUN VALLEY ROAD
Plate 9

END OF THE DAY
Plate 11

SUNRISE—PHI KAPPA CANYON—COPPER BASIN
Plate 10

EARLY MORNING—SUN VALLEY MALL
Plate 12

BIG WOOD RIVER
Plate 15

ROCK GARDEN
Plate 14

LITTLE REDFISH LAKE
Plate 16

PIONEER MOUNTAINS
Plate 17

ASPEN TREES NORTH OF TOWN
Plate 18

WHITE CLOUD MOUNTAINS
Plate 19

CHRISTMAS—ELKHORN
Plate 21

FROZEN SPRUCE NORTH OF TOWN
Plate 20

ELKHORN RESORT
Plate 22

SUN VALLEY LODGE
Plate 23

BOULDER MOUNTAIN TOUR
Plate 24

BOULDER MOUNTAIN TOUR
Plate 25

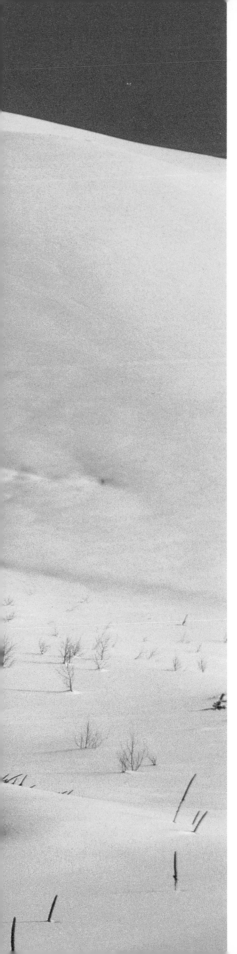

LIMELIGHT
Plate 27

GREYHAWK & CHALLENGER CHAIRLIFTS
Plate 28

DOLLAR CHAIRLIFT
Plate 29

CHALLENGER CHAIRLIFT
Plate 30

RUUD MOUNTAIN CHAIRLIFT
Plate 26

FROM THE TOP
Plate 32

INTO THE BOWLS
Plate 31

BUSTERBACK RANCH
Plate 33

ALONG THE BIG WOOD RIVER
Plate 34

SUN VALLEY LODGE
Plate 35

ELKHORN
Plate 36

BOULDER MOUNTAINS
Plate 38

BUSTERBACK RANCH
Plate 37

STARBURST
Plate 39

FALLING SNOW
Plate 40

BALDY
Plate 41

FROZEN TRAIL CREEK
Plate 43

TRAIL CREEK
Plate 42

THE BIG LOST RIVER RANGE—MACKAY
Plate 44

SUNSET ON THE SNAKE RIVER
Plate 45

MOON OVER THE SAWTOOTHS
Next Page: Plate 46

HELI-SKIING BOULDER MOUNTAINS
Plate 47

CORNER OF MAIN STREET AND
SUN VALLEY ROAD
Plate 48

FROST
Plate 50

SUNRISE—CAMAS PRAIRIE
Plate 49

SUN VALLEY VILLAGE
Plate 51

SILVER PEAK—SMOKY MOUNTAINS
Plate 52

MAIN STREET KETCHUM
Next Page: Plate 53

BEAVER PONDS—BOULDER MOUNTAINS
Plate 57

SUNSET MT. HEYBURN—SAWTOOTH MOUNTAINS
Plate 58

CHRISTMAS ON THE SUN VALLEY MALL
Plate 55

SWIMMING POOL—SUN VALLEY LODGE
Plate 54

FULL MOON—ELKHORN
Plate 56

MORNING SUN SILVER PEAK—SMOKY MOUNTAINS
Plate 59

ROCK GARDEN
Plate 60

ROUND HOUSE
Plate 61

LANE RANCH
Plate 62

ICICLES
Plate 63

LOWER HOLIDAY
Plate 64

FRESH POWDER—SEATTLE RIDGE
Plate 66

BACKSIDE OF SEATTLE RIDGE
Plate 65

TELEMARKING PIONEER MOUNTAINS
Plate 67

FROZEN TRACKS
Plate 68

FISHING THE BIG WOOD RIVER
Plate 69

WOOD RIVER RAINBOW
Plate 70

PIONEER MOUNTAINS
Plate 71

OLD MILK BARN—SUN VALLEY ROAD
Plate 72

REDFISH LAKE CREEK—SAWTOOTH MOUNTAINS
Plate 73

WATERFALL ON HELL ROARING CREEK
Plate 74

SILVER CREEK
Plate 76

FROZEN CAMAS PRAIRIE
Plate 75

ANTELOPE—COPPER BASIN
Plate 77

SPRING IN THE SUN VALLEY HILLS
Plate 78

CAMAS PRAIRIE
Plate 79

BEAR VALLEY CREEK
Plate 80

MULE EARS
Plate 81

THE OLD HIBBARD RANCH
Plate 82

WINDSURFER—REDFISH LAKE
Plate 84

FLY FISHING LITTLE REDFISH LAKE
Plate 83

CAMPING—BOULDER MOUNTAINS
Plate 85

SALMON RIVER—STANLEY
Plate 86

RAFTING THE PAYETTE RIVER
Plate 87

WATER FIGHT—PAYETTE RIVER
Plate 88

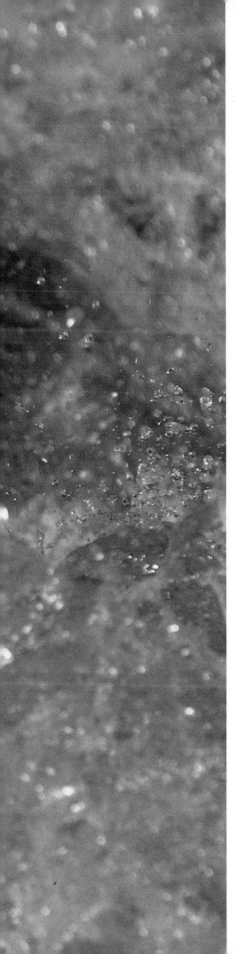

KAYAKING THE PAYETTE RIVER
Plate 90

KAYAKING THE SNAKE RIVER
Plate 89

PIONEER MOUNTAINS FROM TIMMERMAN HILL
Plate 91

WHITE CLOUD MOUNTAINS FROM COPPER BASIN
Plate 92

IN THE HELL ROARING BASIN ABOVE
IMOGENE LAKE
Plate 93

BOULDER CITY
Plate 94

SHEEP—SAWTOOTH SUMMER RANGE
Plate 96

IRRIGATION—BELLEVUE TRIANGLE
Plate 95

SUNSET POINT OF ROCKS—SILVER CREEK
Plate 97

FULL MOON OVER SILVER CREEK
Plate 98

FLY FISHING SILVER CREEK
Plate 99

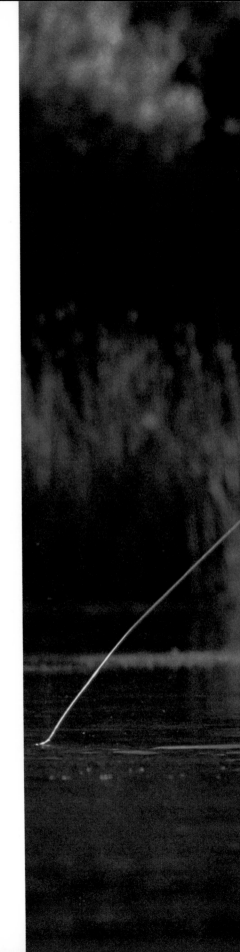

FLY FISHING SILVER CREEK
Plate 100

JOGGER—ADAMS GULCH
Plate 101

SWIMMING A HIGH MOUNTAIN LAKE
IN THE SAWTOOTHS
Plate 102

THE BIG LOST RIVER RANGE—MACKAY
Plate 104

KANE LAKE—PIONEER MOUNTAINS
Plate 103

WARM SPRINGS GOLF COURSE
Plate 105

PRACTICE TEE—ELKHORN
Plate 106

SUN VALLEY INN
Plate 107

SAND TRAP—SUN VALLEY GOLF COURSE
Plate 108

ROAD BIKING—SHOSHONE
Plate 116

SWANS—SUN VALLEY MALL
Plate 115

DOCKS—REDFISH RESORT
Plate 118

REDFISH LAKE
Plate 117

LITTLE REDFISH LAKE
Next Page: Plate 119

BIKING—GANNETT
Plate 121

BEAVER PONDS—BOULDER MOUNTAINS
Plate 120

RAINBOW TROUT—LOVING CREEK
Plate 122

"THE CATCH"—LOVING CREEK
Plate 123

FISHING—SALMON RIVER
Next Page: Plate 124

SILVER CREEK
Plate 125

BALDY FROM TRAIL CREEK
Plate 126

WARM SPRINGS ROAD—BOARD RANCH
Plate 127

SUN VALLEY GOLF COURSE
Plate 128

ASPEN TREES—BOULDER MOUNTAINS
Next Page: Plate 129

WARM SPRINGS CREEK
Plate 131

OLD SCHOOL—CORRAL
Plate 130

SULLIVAN'S SLOUGH—SILVER CREEK
Plate 132

CANADIAN GEESE—SILVER CREEK
Plate 133

ASPEN TREES—WARM SPRINGS
Plate 134

TRAIL CREEK
Plate 135

NORTH FORK OF THE BIG LOST RIVER
Plate 136

ASPEN GROVE IN THE BOULDER MOUNTAINS
Plate 137

TOP OF SILVER CREEK IN THE
BOULDER MOUNTAINS
Plate 138

SUNSET ON THE SNAKE RIVER—HAGERMAN
Plate 139

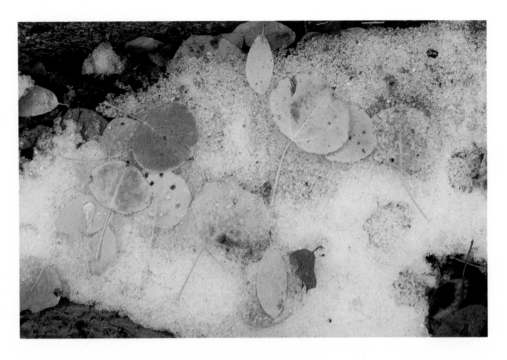

FROZEN ASPEN LEAVES
Plate 140

BIG WOOD RIVER
Plate 141

SULLIVAN'S SLOUGH
Plate 143

FLY FISHING SULLIVAN'S SLOUGH
Plate 142

MALLARDS—STATE PRESERVE—HAGERMAN
Plate 144

MALLARDS COMING INTO CORN—HAGERMAN
Plate 145

ELK HUNTING—HEADWATERS OF
THE SALMON RIVER
Plate 146

ELK CAMP—WHITE CLOUD MOUNTAINS
Plate 147

PETTIT LAKE
Plate 148

FISHING LITTLE REDFISH LAKE
Plate 149

SUN VALLEY POND
Next Page: Plate 150

M O D E L S

Photo: Gretchen Palmer

ABOUT THE PHOTOGRAPHER

David Stoecklein is sought by international corporations including Kodak, Coca-Cola, Chrysler and Fila for his photography. Magazines and ad agencies around the world use his outdoor lifestyle images. Though his assignments require that he travel often, he still photographs in Sun Valley whenever possible. He lives in Sun Valley with his wife Mary and their children Drew, Taylor and Colby.

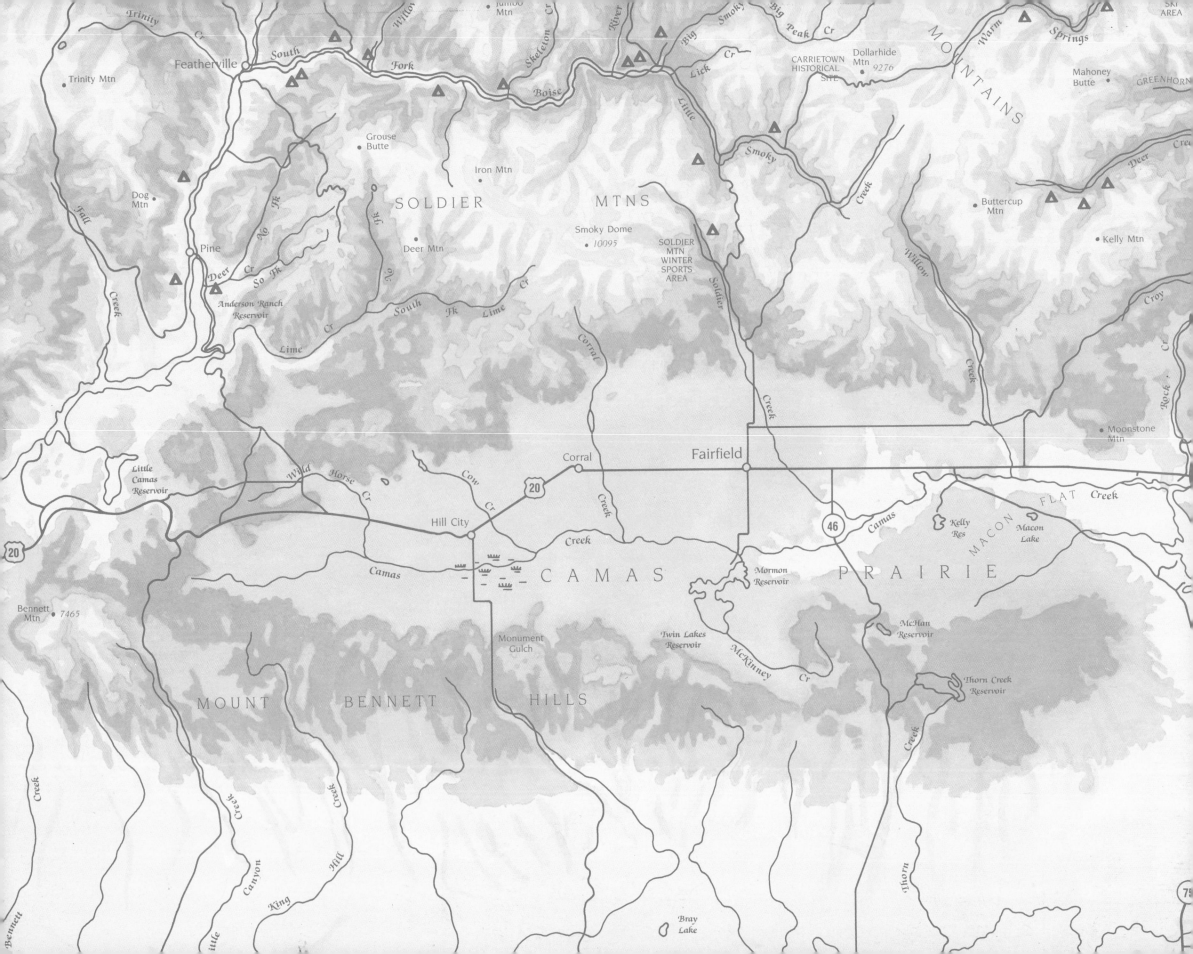